GEOGRAPHY OF THE WORLD

NORTH AMERICA

By Dana Meachen Rau

THE CHILD'S WORLD®
CHANHASSEN, MINNESOTA

Published in the United States of America by The Child's World®
P.O. Box 326, Chanhassen, MN 55317-0326
800-599-READ
www.childsworld.com

Photo Credits: Cover: Darrell Gulin/Corbis; Animals Animals/Earth Scenes: 6 (Jim Steinberg), 7 (Ruth Cole), 9 (Richard La Val), 12 (James Watt), 13 (Phil Degginger), 18 (Momatiuk Eastcott); Corbis: 8 (Scott T. Smith), 9 (Wolfgang Kaehler), 11 (Richard Hamilton Smith), 17 (Royalty Free), 20 (Joe McDonald), 21 (Rob Howard), 24 (AFP), 27; Picture Desk: 16 (Travelsite/Neil Setchfield), 23 (Art Archive/Biblioteca Nacional Madrid/Dagli Orti).

The Child's World®: Mary Berendes, Publishing Director
Editorial Directions, Inc.: E. Russell Primm, Editorial Director; Pam Rosenberg, Line Editor; Katie Marsico, Assistant Editor; Olivia Nellums, Editorial Assistant; Susan Hindman, Copy Editor; Elizabeth K. Martin, Proofreader; Ann Grau Duvall, Peter Garnham, Carol Yehling, Fact Checkers; Dr. Charles Maynara, Professor of Geography, Radford University, Radford, Virginia, Subject Consultant; Tim Griffin/IndexServ, Indexer; Cian Loughlin O'Day, Photo Researcher; Elizabeth K. Martin, Photo Selector; XNR Productions, Inc., Cartographer

Copyright © 2004 by The Child's World®
All rights reserved. No part of this book may be reproduced or utilized in any form or by any means without written permission from the publisher.

Library of Congress Cataloging-in-Publication Data
Rau, Dana Meachen, 1971–
  North America / by Dana Meachen Rau.
    p. cm. — (Geography of the world series)
Summary: Introduces the geography, topography, and climate of the continent of North America. Includes bibliographical references and index.
  ISBN 1-59296-061-8 (lib. bdg. : alk. paper)
 1. North America—Juvenile literature. 2. North America—Geography—Juvenile literature. [1. North America—Geography.] I. Title. II. Series.
E38.5.R38 2004
917—dc21   2003006343

Table of Contents

CHAPTER ONE
4 Where Is North America?

CHAPTER TWO
9 How Did North America Come to Be?

CHAPTER THREE
13 What Makes North America Special?

CHAPTER FOUR
17 What Animals and Plants Are Found in North America?

CHAPTER FIVE
21 Who Lives in North America?

CHAPTER SIX
25 What Is North America Like Today?

28 Glossary

29 A North American Almanac

30 North America in the News

31 How to Learn More about North America

32 Index

CHAPTER ONE

Where Is North America?

Earth can be divided into two halves called the Eastern Hemisphere and the Western Hemisphere. North America is found in the Western Hemisphere, along with the continent of South America.

North America is located in the northern part of the Western Hemisphere. It stretches from about 170° west **longitude** to 20° west longitude and from about 83° north **latitude** to 7° north latitude. Most of North America sits between the line of latitude around the North Pole called the Arctic Circle and the line of latitude a little above the center of the globe called the tropic of Cancer. Lines of latitude help us measure how far north or south of the **equator** a place is located.

> **THE ROCKY MOUNTAINS**
> The Rocky Mountain range that stretches down the western side of the continent includes the Alaska, Coast, Rocky, Sierra Nevada, and Sierra Madre Mountains.

A physical map of North America

To the north, North America is bordered by the Arctic Ocean. The Atlantic Ocean lies on its eastern shores, and the Pacific Ocean on its western shores. The southern border of North America is a tiny strip of land only about 30 miles (50 kilometers) wide between the Central American country of Panama and the country of Colombia in the continent of South America.

North America has two major mountain ranges. The Appalachian Mountains lie along the eastern part of

THE MISSISSIPPI RIVER SYSTEM

The largest river system in North America is the Mississippi system. This includes the Mississippi, Missouri, and Ohio Rivers and all of the smaller rivers that flow into them, called tributaries. These rivers act like a giant drain for much of the continent.

The White River in Colorado runs through part of North America's longest mountain range, the Rocky Mountains.

The warm coasts of the Caribbean Islands attract many tourists every year.

the continent, in the United States. The much taller Rocky Mountain range runs down the western side of North America, all the way from Alaska to Central America.

Because North America is so large, it has many types of **climates.** Some areas, especially those in the north, are cold throughout the year. The majority of the continent has warm summers and cold winters. The southern United States, Mexico, and Central America are mild or hot all year long. The islands of the Caribbean are very hot and tropical.

The land, too, is very different across the continent. Most of Greenland is always covered with ice. Canada also has very cold and unlivable areas where no trees can grow, called the **tundra.** The rest of the continent is filled with a mix of lowlands, high mountains, flat plains, thick forests, and dry deserts.

Autumn in the tundra along Kesugi Ridge in Denali National Park, Alaska

CHAPTER TWO

How Did North America Come to Be?

North America is one of seven large areas of land that cover Earth. These land areas are called continents. North America includes Greenland, Canada, the United States, Mexico, the countries of Central America, and the islands of the Caribbean Sea.

North America has a wide range of climates, from the cold, coastal fishing communities of Greenland to the humid, tropical rain forests of Costa Rica (above right)

THE CONTINENTS

In order from largest to smallest, the continents are:
- Asia
- Africa
- North America
- South America
- Antarctica
- Europe
- Australia

Each of these places is very unique. But they are all a part of the North American continent.

North America is very wide to the north and very narrow to the south. It was not always shaped like it is today. One must look back about 200 million years to see how North America was formed.

Many scientists believe that long ago, all of the land areas on Earth were clumped together as one large mass of land. This land was called Pangaea. Over time, Pangaea broke into pieces, forming the continents. The continents slowly moved into the places where they are found today.

About 600 million years ago, a shallow sea covered much of the land that became North America. Scientists know this because they

These bluffs over Lake Superior were formed when glaciers melted long ago.

have found **fossils** of sea animals in the inner part of the continent. This sea disappeared. Then, about 230 million years ago, mountains formed on the continent. About 2.5 million years ago, much of North America was covered by huge sheets of ice called glaciers. As the glaciers covered the land, they carved out paths. When the glaciers finally

THE CHANGING EARTH

Earth is changing all the time. Weather and rivers change the way the land looks by erosion. Volcanoes are still active. Earthquakes cause the land to shift and move. Over the next millions of years, the continents will change their positions even more. This is called continental drift.

melted away, they left behind channels and craters that became rivers and lakes.

Other parts of North America were formed by volcanoes. The Hawaiian Islands and the Caribbean Islands were formed this way.

Hot lava flows from an erupting volcano.

CHAPTER THREE

What Makes North America Special?

Many places in North America make it an amazing place to visit. The highest point on the continent is Mount McKinley. It is a mountain in the center of the Alaska Range in Alaska.

At more than 20,000 feet (6,100 meters), Mount McKinley in Alaska is North America's tallest mountain.

A political map of North America

While Mount McKinley is tall, another feature of North America is very deep. It is the Grand Canyon in Arizona. The Grand Canyon was carved by the Colorado River. For about 6 million years, the river has flowed through the canyon, carving it deeper and deeper.

One of the most unique features of North America is the Great Lakes. There are five of them—Erie, Huron, Michigan, Ontario, and Superior. Lake Michigan is completely within the United States. The other four lakes form part of the border between the United States and Canada. The Great Lakes form the largest area of freshwater in the world. In fact, Lake Superior is the largest freshwater lake on Earth.

Niagara Falls is one of the most beautiful sites in North America. It is made up of two waterfalls—the Horseshoe Falls and the

> **NATIONAL PARKS**
>
> People want to be sure the beautiful lands of North America stay that way. There are many national parks in North America. These parks are areas protected by the governments of each country. No one can build or farm on them. They are set aside for people to visit and enjoy. The United States has more than 123,000 square miles (318,568 sq km) of land set aside for national parks. In Canada, more than 85,000 square miles (220,148 sq km) of land are used for national parks.

The Maid of the Mist *gives tourists an up-close look at Niagara Falls.*

THE PANAMA CANAL

One man-made feature of North America that is quite a sight is the Panama Canal. It was built between 1904 and 1914 on a 10-mile (16-km) strip of land across Panama by workers from all over the world. It connects the Atlantic and Pacific Oceans.

American Falls. They lie in the Niagara River, which connects Lake Erie and Lake Ontario. People love to visit this site, where they can take tours behind the falling water or watch the water crash from a boat on the Niagara River.

CHAPTER FOUR

What Animals and Plants Are Found in North America?

With so many different types of land and weather, it is no wonder that there are many kinds of animals and plants across the continent.

Cypress trees grow well in the wet and humid environment of the Louisiana bayou.

A musk ox sheds its heavy winter coat.

THE SAGUARO

The saguaro is a type of cactus that grows in the southwestern deserts of North America. It is very tall with long spikes across its surface. Insects and bats drink the sweet nectar of its flowers. Birds even dig out holes in the cactus and make homes there.

In the cold north, musk oxen, with their warm wool and hair, roam the lands of Greenland. Caribou, polar bears, puffins, hares, and foxes have also found ways to adapt to this harsh, icy land. Walrus, seals, and whales swim in the cold waters. This region has very few trees. But there are many shrubs and smaller plants, including flowers. Mosses and lichens grow on rocks.

Two very common animals in Canada are the beaver and the moose, which live in the forests that cover much of the country. The mountains of North America are home to sheep and goats that can scale their high peaks. Tall redwood trees grow in the west. These forests, as well as many others in North America, are home to squirrels, raccoons, deer, and many other woodland creatures. The dry plains, with hardy plants such as tumbleweed, are home to two animals that do not live on any other continent—the pronghorn and the coyote.

Not many plants grow in North

> **ENDANGERED ANIMALS**
> Some animals in North America are in danger of disappearing forever. They are considered endangered. Animals such as the bald eagle and the gray wolf are two of the many animals that need protection. The governments and people of North American countries are doing what they can to save them.

The great roadrunner relies on its speed to keep away from hungry predators.

America's deserts. But one very strong plant is the cactus. These spiky plants can be small or very large. Roadrunners and rattlesnakes live on the dry ground of the desert.

In the more tropical areas of the southern part of the continent, the plant and animal life changes even more. Fruit trees grow here, as well as colorful flowers. Bright pink flamingoes wade in the water, and monkeys swing from the tree branches.

CHAPTER FIVE

Who Lives in North America?

Historians believe that somewhere between 15,000 and 35,000 years ago, the first people came to North America. They crossed a land bridge that connected Asia to North America. These groups, the first Native Americans, settled in various places, from the cold north to the warm south.

Historians think that early American peoples, such as the Inuit, came from Asia to Alaska more than 10,000 years ago.

WHY WAS THERE A LAND BRIDGE?

Long ago, a land bridge connected Asia with North America. At the time, much of Earth's water was frozen in glaciers. So the land between the two continents was above water. As the glaciers melted, the land bridge was slowly covered up.

In the 1400s, explorers from Spain crossed the Atlantic Ocean. Their boats landed in Central America. Their armies were much stronger than those of the Native Americans, and they took over much of the land.

People from France and Great Britain made the Atlantic trip in the 1600s. They moved into the area of North America that is now Canada and the United States.

The Spanish brought Africans to the Caribbean islands to work as slaves. Africans were also sold to farmers in the United States to work.

In the late 1800s and early 1900s, millions of **immigrants** from European countries came to North America's eastern coast. Many immigrants from Asian countries, such as China and Japan,

Spanish explorer Hernán Cortéz conquered the Aztecs and claimed their empire for Spain. He is shown above meeting the Aztec woman who served as his interpreter.

arrived on the western shores.

Today, most people of North America have European roots. Many Canadians were originally from France.

AMERICAN INDIANS

The cultures of North American Indian groups developed in response to the type of land they lived on. The Inuit began wearing snowshoes to get around in the snowy north. The bows and arrows of the Plains Indians were first developed to hunt the bison that were plentiful in their region.

The people of Mexico and Central America hold on to the Spanish culture of their past. Most Caribbeans can trace their origin to Africa. In some countries, such as Mexico and Guatemala, Native Americans make up at least one-third of the population. Many Native Americans have either blended with other cultures or are trying to hold on to their traditions in a changing world.

Mayans of Guatemala worship Earth in a traditional ritual.

CHAPTER SIX

What Is North America Like Today?

Today, people live and work all over North America. Some lands are almost unlivable, such as the icy north, the high mountains, and the dry deserts. Many people live along the eastern coast between Massachusetts and Washington, D.C. A lot of people also live around the Great Lakes and in southern California. Mexico City, Mexico, is the largest city in North America.

The United States and Canada make products for many other countries. They produce computers, automobiles, petroleum, electronic equipment, steel, and many other goods.

Other parts of North America, such

> **LARGE CITIES**
> Some of the world's largest cities are in North America. Mexico City and its surrounding populations make up the second largest urban area in the world, with about 18,000,000 people. New York City is the fifth largest, with 16,650,000 people. Los Angeles, California, is the seventh largest, with 13,140,000.

as Mexico and other Central American countries, are actually some of the poorest places in the world. Many of the people there have little money and food to live.

The land in the center of North America is rich farmland. Here, farmers are able to grow many crops, such as corn, wheat, cotton, and potatoes. They also raise **livestock,** such as cows and pigs. In Mexico, one out of four people is a farmer. Farmers in Mexico and throughout Central America grow coffee, sugarcane, and bananas in the tropical climate. North America produces the most food of any continent. It sells much of this food to other countries.

Visitors to North America can see many different scenes. In the mild weather of Mexico, they might see shoppers in

EASY TO GET AROUND
North America has many railroads, highways, and airline systems. This makes it very easy for people to get from place to place. People travel across the continent for business trips, to visit family and friends, or for vacations.

Farms, such as this one in Wisconsin, dot the countryside of the midwestern United States and Canada.

open-air markets. From above, the middle of the United States looks like a patchwork of fields growing crops. In large cities, such as New York, Montreal, and Mexico City, people and cars fill the busy streets with activity. Visitors to the warm coastal resorts of the southern United States, Mexico, and other Central American countries will see vacationers enjoying the sun and water sports. Fishing boats are docked on Greenland's icy shores. Totem poles in Canada are a reminder of the first people who walked the land of the great North American continent.

Glossary

canal (kuh-NAL) A canal is a man-made waterway that connects two large bodies of water.

climates (KLYE-mits) Climates are the usual weather conditions found in various regions.

equator (i-KWAY-tur) The equator is an imaginary line that circles Earth half-way between the North and South Poles.

erosion (ih-ROH-zhuhn) Erosion is the breaking down of land by water and wind.

fossils (FOSS-uhlz) Fossils are the remains of plants and animals from millions of years ago.

immigrants (IM-uh-gruhnts) Immigrants are people who leave their country and go to a new country to live.

latitude (LAT-uh-tood) Latitude is the position of a place on the globe as it is measured in degrees north or south of the equator.

livestock (LIVE-stok) Livestock are animals that are raised on farms or ranches.

longitude (LON-juh-tood) Longitude is the position of a place on the globe as it is measured in degrees east or west of an imaginary line known as the prime meridian. The prime meridian runs through the Greenwich Observatory in London, England, and is sometimes called the Greenwich Meridian.

tundra (TUHN-druh) The tundra is a large area in Arctic regions where no trees grow and the soil under the ground is permanently frozen.

A North American Almanac

Location on the Globe:
Longitude: 170° west to 20° west
Latitude: 83° north to 7° north

Greatest distance from north to south: 4,500 miles (7,200 km)

Greatest distance from east to west: 4,000 miles (6,400 km)

Borders: Arctic Ocean, Pacific Ocean, Atlantic Ocean, Denmark Strait, Bering Strait, Colombia, South America

Total Area: 9,347,000 square miles (24,208,000 sq km)

Highest Point: Mount McKinley, 20,320 feet (6,194 m) above sea level

Lowest Point: Death Valley, 282 feet (86 m) below sea level

Number of Countries on the Continent: 23

Major Mountain Ranges: Alaska, Appalachian, Cascade, Coast, Rocky, Sierra Madre, Sierra Nevada

Major Deserts: Chihuahuan, Colorado, Great Basin, Mojave, Painted, Sonoran, Vizcaino, Yuma

Major Rivers: Arkansas, Colorado, Columbia, Fraser, Mackenzie, Mississippi, Missouri, Nelson, Ohio, Rio Grande, St. Lawrence, Yukon

Major Lakes: Athabasca, Erie, Great Bear, Great Salt, Great Slave, Huron, Michigan, Nicaragua, Ontario, Superior, Winnipeg

Major Cities:
Mexico City, Mexico
New York, United States
Los Angeles, United States
Chicago, United States
Toronto, Canada
Montreal, Canada

Languages: English, Spanish, and French are the major languages. Immigrants to the countries of North America from around the world speak many other languages.

Population: 480,633,000 (estimated 2000)

Religions: Christianity, Judaism, Islam, Buddhism, Hinduism

Mineral Resources: Silver, natural gas, nickel, phosphate rock, potash, copper, crude oil, lead, coal

North America in the News

170 million B.C.	North America breaks away from the present-day continents of Europe and Africa.
20,000 B.C.	Small groups of hunter-gatherers migrate across the Bering land bridge from Asia to North America.
A.D. 982	Erik the Red settles in Greenland after being banished from Iceland.
1400s	Europeans begin their explorations of North America.
1500s – 1600s	Europeans from England, France, and Spain start colonies in North America.
1521	Spanish conquistador Hernán Cortéz conquers the Aztecs and takes control of their empire in present-day Mexico.
1534	French explorer Jacques Cartier explores the Gulf of St. Lawrence and claims it for France.
1607	Jamestown, the first permanent British settlement in North America, is founded.
1680	Pueblo Indians in New Mexico revolt and succeed in overthrowing Spanish rule.
1721	Hans Egede, a missionary from the united kingdom of Denmark-Norway establishes a trading company and Lutheran mission on Greenland.
1754 – 1763	The French and Indian War is fought as the British and French battle for control of North America.
1775 – 1783	The American Revolutionary War is fought and England's 13 North American colonies gain their independence, becoming the United States of America.
1821	Mexico gains its independence from Spain.
1861 – 1865	A civil war is fought between the U.S. government and 11 Southern states that broke away from the Union and formed the Confederate States of America.
1867	The British parliament passes the British North America Act uniting the colonies of Nova Scotia, New Brunswick, and Canada as a single dominion named Canada.
1906	A huge earthquake occurs on April 18. San Francisco experiences severe damage, including a fire that destroys its central business district.
1914	The Panama Canal is completed, making it possible to sail from the east coast of North America to the west coast of North America without sailing around the continent of South America.
1980	Mount Saint Helens erupts in one of the biggest volcanic explosions ever recorded in North America.

How to Learn More about North America

At the Library

Barlas, Bob, and Norman Tompsett. *Canada.*
Milwaukee, Wisc.: Gareth Stevens Publishing, 1998.

Miles, Kelly. *Scholastic Atlas of the World.* New York: Scholastic Reference, 2001.

Murdoch, David, and Elizabeth Baquedano. *American Peoples.*
New York: Dorling Kindersley, 1996.

Stein, R. Conrad. *Mexico.* Danbury, Conn.: Children's Press, 1998.

On the Web

Visit our home page for lots of links about North America:
http://www.childsworld.com/links.html
Note to Parents, Teachers, and Librarians: We routinely verify our Web links to make sure they're safe, active sites—so encourage your readers to check them out!

Places to Visit or Contact

THE FIELD MUSEUM
*To tour the museum's permanent exhibits on
the natural history and cultures of North America*
1400 South Lake Shore Drive
Chicago, IL 60605
312/922-9410

NATIONAL GEOGRAPHIC SOCIETY
To write for information about its many educational programs and publications
1145 17th Street N.W.
Washington, DC 20036-4688
800/647-5463

Index

Alaska Range, 13
animal life, 17–18, 19
Appalachian Mountains, 6–7
Arctic Ocean, 5
Atlantic Ocean, 5

cactuses, 20
Canada, 8, 15, 19, 22, 25, 27
Caribbean Islands, 12
Central America, 6, 7–8, 22, 24, 26, 27
climate, 7, 26–27
Colorado River, 14–15

deserts, 20, 25

ethnic groups, 22–24

farming, 26, 27
fossils, 11
France, 22

glaciers, 11–12, 22
Grand Canyon, 14–15

Great Britain, 22
Great Lakes, 15, 16, 25
Greenland, 8, 18, 27

Hawaiian Islands, 12
Horseshoe Falls, 15

immigration, 22–23

lakes, 15
land bridge, 21
livestock, 26

manufacturing, 25
Mexico, 7, 24, 25, 26–27
Mount McKinley, 13
mountains, 6–7, 11, 13, 19, 25

Native Americans, 21, 24, 27
Niagara Falls, 15–16
Niagara River, 16

Ohio River, 6

Pacific Ocean, 5, 16
Panama Canal, 16
Pangaea, 10
plant life, 17, 18–19, 20
population, 25

rivers, 6, 12, 14–15, 16
Rocky Mountains, 4, 7

saguaro cactus, 18
Sierra Madre, 4
Sierra Nevada, 4
size, 10
Spain, 22

transportation, 26
tundra region, 8

United States, 7, 15, 22, 25, 27
urban areas, 25

volcanoes, 12

About the Author

Dana Meachen Rau is a children's book author, editor, and illustrator. She has written more than 70 books, including nonfiction, biographies, early readers, and historical fiction. A graduate of Trinity College in Hartford, Connecticut, Dana is happiest when she is drinking a cup of hot cocoa, sitting on the couch, and holding her pad and pen. She works from her home office in Burlington, Connecticut, where she lives with her husband, Chris, and children, Charlie and Allison.